LITTLE BIG BOOK

# THE CAT FAMILY

SUE NASH

Editor: Trisha Pike   Designer: Jacky Cowdrey
Picture Researcher: Kathy Brandt

**Purnell**

**Above: Miacis was the ancestor of cats and lived 40 million years ago.**

# 1 THE FIRST CATS

Cats have lived on the Earth for many more years than men. Even so, there was a time when there were no cats at all in the world.

About 40 million years ago there were no cats like the ones we see today. But there was an animal called Miacis. It was a small creature with short legs, a long body and a long tail. It looked rather like a weasel and hunted for its food. After millions of years Miacis developed, or evolved, into a bigger and stronger animal in order to survive. This new animal was the civet. It looks more catlike than Miacis.

After millions of years more, the primitive civet evolved into all the

**Above: After Miacis came the civet which had longer legs and looked more like a cat.**

different members of the cat family—the lion, the tiger, the leopard, the cheetah, the jaguar, the lynx and the wildcat. The civet developed into these different kinds of cat because each kind was the fittest to survive in the surroundings where it lived.

Much later, some of the wild-cats evolved into our tame Tabby cat. So the Miacis was a very important animal. In a sense it was the very first cat to live on Earth.

**Below: This saber-tooth tiger is one kind of cat that no longer exists.**

**Left: The lion, the tiger and the pet cat are all true cats and come from the same family.**

# 2 LIVING WITH PEOPLE

How did the wild-cat become the domestic cat which we keep as a pet today? It was not just tamed. Wild-cats are very difficult to tame, but even if you succeeded in taming one, its kittens would still be wild-cats—fierce untamed animals.

It took thousands of years for some of the wild-cats to turn gradually into domestic cats. It probably started gradually when cats found warmth and comfort by crouching near people's fires. They found food as well, from the meat which was cooked on the fires'

**Above: Cats were sacred to the people of Egypt. They mummified the bodies of cats to preserve them after they had died.**

**Below: The Egyptian cat goddess kills a snake for her brother.**

flames.

We do not know exactly when or how cats and people became friends but we know for certain that domestic cats were living in Ancient Egypt 4,000 years ago. In those days the Egyptians grew more grain than anyone else in the world. A lot of this grain was eaten by rats, mice and birds. The Egyptian farmers were only too glad to have cats to help them kill these pests.

The Egyptian cats were like our Tabby cats. They were quite small and their fur either dusty yellow or gray. They had black stripes on their legs and tails.

**Below: Cats were very useful to the Ancient Egyptians, because they killed the animals that ate the grain.**

## 3 WILD-CATS

**Above: Wild-cats can be found only in forests and mountains, hunting alone.**

Only some of the wild-cats developed into domestic cats. The rest remained just as wild as ever.

They are still found in North America, Scotland and parts of Europe. They live in rocky, wooded places and are not often seen. They hunt mice, voles, rabbits and birds for food. If there are fish nearby they will stand in the water to catch them with their claws.

Wild-cats are much bigger and heavier than domesticated cats.

Their tails are shorter and thicker and not shaped to a point like those of pet cats. Their coloring is like a Tabby cat's. They have black markings on their heads, faces, backs and legs. Their fur is very thick. As they live out in the open they need a heavy coat for warmth.

Some domesticated cats spend all their time wandering around the streets or the countryside. These cats are strays which have no owners to look after them. They have to find their own food and shelter as wildcats do. But they are not wildcats. You can easily make them pets.

**Below: At a quick glance this wildcat looks very much like a Tabby cat.**

**Below: This domesticated cat is a stray because it has no owner.**

## 4  CAT'S RELATIVES

Although the animals in the cat family can look and behave very differently from one another, they all have certain things in common.

They all have very sharp teeth. This is because they all eat meat as their main food. They all hunt for their food and are all good at running. They all have soft pads on their feet to help them move quietly.

They all have very sharp claws. These help the cats when hunting and climbing trees. Their claws cannot be seen all of the time. This is

**Above: The cheetah runs the fastest.**

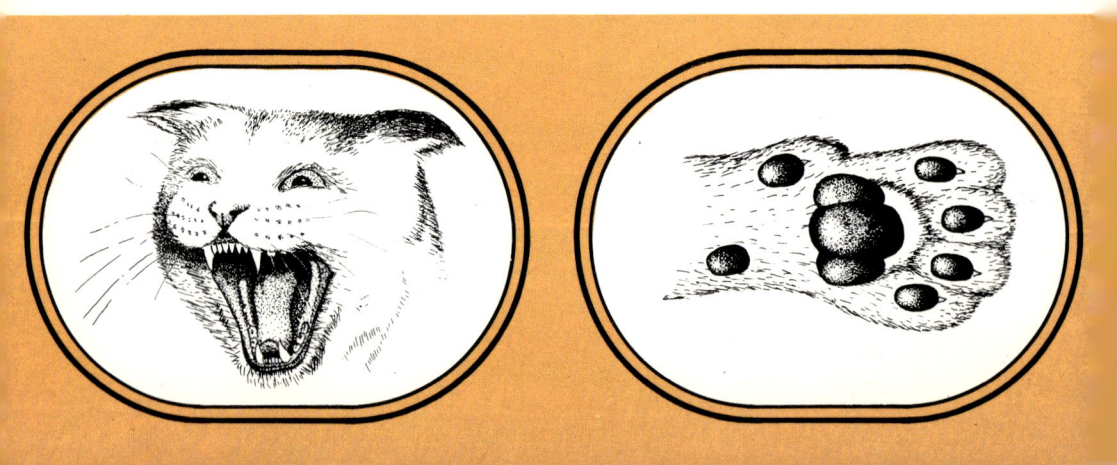

**Below: The lion is the king of the beasts.**

because a cat can hide them away in a fold of skin called a sheath. When the cat needs to use them it pushes them out of their sheaths. The only cat which is unable to do this is the cheetah. All cats have four toes on their back feet and five toes on their front feet.

There are over 50 different members of the cat family. Perhaps the one which looks most different from all the rest is the male lion. It has short, smooth fur over its body but very long hair on its head and shoulders. There is also a long tuft of hair on the tip of its tail.

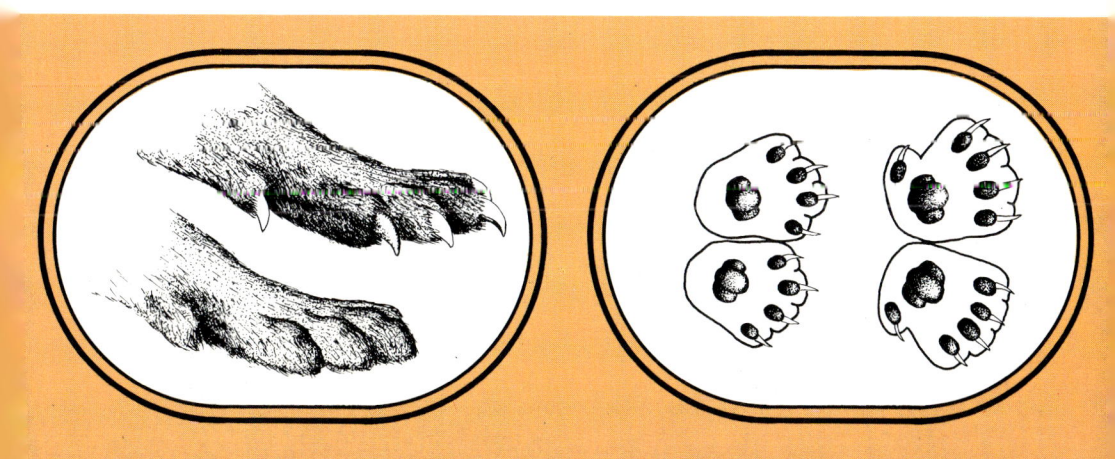

**Above: An angry cat arches its back and its fur stands on end.**

## 5  THE CAT'S SENSES

When a pet cat is happy and contented it makes a purring noise. When it is angry it arches its back and hisses. It does this to make itself appear as big and fierce as possible. It tries to scare off its enemy.

A cat has long whiskers on either side of its face and sticking out above its eyes. These whiskers help the cat to feel its way in the dark.

Although cats are color-blind, they have very sharp eyesight. In darkness their pupils (the black parts of their eyes) grow larger. This lets in as much light as possible to

**Left: If a cat falls it can twist around in midair to land safely with all four paws on the ground.**

help the cat to see at night.

If a cat falls from a tree or a fence it will usually land on its feet. Cats have a good sense of balance. They can tell exactly which way to turn so that they land without hurting themselves. However, small children must be very careful not to drop a cat because they are not tall enough to give the animal enough height in which to right itself.

A cat is able to twist its ears about to pick up the direction of any sound it has heard. Like dogs, cats can hear certain sounds which people cannot hear.

**Below: On the left the pupil is small. On the right it is much larger.**

# 6 SHORT HAIR

Until 100 years or so ago, all pet cats were Tabbies, like those in Ancient Egypt. Then people started to breed cats to get a special color or length of hair. We now have many breeds of domestic cats. They can be divided into two main classes: short-haired cats and long-haired cats.

There are two kinds of short-haired cats. One is the Domestic Short-hair. These cats have wide-apart eyes and ears and short, blunt noses.

The Tabby cats belong to the

**Above: The head of a Tabby.**

**Below: Two cartoon Siameses.**

**Below: A Tabby with black circular markings.**

Domestic Short-hair group. Some Tabby cats have black markings which form circles around their legs and bodies. Others have black patches which make a butterfly shape across their shoulders.

The second kind of short-haired cat is known as the Oriental Short-hair. Their faces are long and pointed. Their ears are quite large and pointed and they have almond-shaped eyes.

The Siamese cats are Oriental Short-hairs. The usual color of the Siamese is cream with brown face, ears, legs and tail.

**Above: The front view and the side view of a Siamese cat's face.**

**Left: This Tabby has a butterfly-shaped marking across its shoulders.**

**Above: All long-haired cats have silky, long, flowing coats.**

**Below: This beautiful Persian is the trademark of a carpet manufacturer.**

# 7   LONG HAIR

Long-haired cats have very long fur over their faces and bodies. They look much heavier than short-haired cats as their legs and bodies are shorter and thicker. They have bushy tails which are often called "brushes". Their heads are wide and round. The fur on their necks is very thick. The Persian, Himalayan, Chinchilla, Birman and Tortoise Shell are all long-haired cats.

In Mongolia, Tibet and Asia there is a wild-cat called the Pallas Cat. It lives and hunts among the rocks. Its fur is thick and long. Because of the way it looks, many people thought that the Persian could be a great-grandchild of the Pallas Cat. This is unlikely because the body and face markings are quite different.

The Chinchilla is thought to be the most beautiful of cats. It has long, white fur with each hair tipped with black. This makes the fur look as though it is sparkling.

Persian cats are different from each other only in the color of their fur and eyes. Their coats can be any color. Their eyes may be green, blue, orange or yellow.

**Above: The Pallas cat is a wild-cat.**

**Below: One of the oldest breeds is a black Persian.**

# 8 UNUSUAL CATS

A very odd-looking cat is the Peke-faced Persian. Its head and face is like that of a Pekinese dog. It has a flat nose and wrinkles of skin over its cheeks.

White cats with blue eyes are nearly always deaf. It is very unusual to find a cat of this coloring that has normal hearing.

There are some types of cats which are different from those in the short-hair group and also those in the long-hair group. Because of this these types of cats each belong to a group of their own.

The most famous of these is the Manx. This cat has no tail. A tail

**Above: This Peke-faced Persian looks as though it has a pushed-in nose.**

**Below: The Manx cat comes from the Isle of Man and it has no tail.**

helps a cat keep its balance when climbing trees. The Manx cat therefore does not enjoy climbing as it cannot balance very well. The back legs of the Manx cat are very long. This makes it walk with a sort of hopping movement. Other cats have a smooth, graceful stride.

Rex is the name given to a type of cat with only a very thin layer of fur. The fur is curly and looks almost like wool. There is another cat which has so little fur that it looks bald. This is the Mexican Hairless Cat.

**Above: A white cat with both eyes blue is usually deaf. As this cat has only one blue eye, it can hear quite normally.**

**Below: The Rex cat has a silky curly coat and makes a good pet because it does not molt.**

Above: A kitten should have its own warm, dry bed. Give it a basket lined with paper and a blanket.

## 9 KITTENS

A kitten is ready to leave its mother when it is six weeks old. Up until this time it has always been with its brothers and sisters. When a kitten goes to a new home it feels lonely for the first few days. If it is given lots of love and attention it will soon settle happily to its new life.

There are some important things to remember when caring for a kitten. It must be taken to a vet to be immunized. This will stop your pet from catching any serious illnesses. A very young kitten's stomach is very

Above: These little kittens will soon be ready to leave and go to their own homes.

**Above: A kitten needs a litter box big enough for it to sit in. It should be metal or plastic with sand.**

**Below: A kitten loves playthings and they will give it exercise as well as fun.**

small, so it cannot eat much food at a time. It needs to eat about four small meals a day. It should have its own box or basket for sleeping in. This must be kept clean and dry.

House-training is also important. Put a tray of sand on the floor. Take one of the kitten's paws and gently scrape at the sand with it. The kitten will soon learn that this is where it must go to toilet. The tray must be cleaned every day or otherwise the kitten will not want to use it.

Kittens will love playing with balls and pieces of string, but as they are still babies they need a lot of rest.

# 10 AROUND THE HOUSE

**Above: Everyone knows how cats like warmth. This Abyssinian cat is lying on a warm wall and basking in the sun.**

When a kitten grows into a cat it will not need human company quite so much. It will still enjoy being played with and talked to. It will still like to curl up on somebody's lap, but it will often want to be by itself.

Everyone knows that cats hunt birds and mice. So, any small pets must be kept out of the cat's way.

Cats love being warm and comfortable. They like to lie as close to a fire as they can. In summer they often stretch out in the sunshine. They enjoy climbing trees and will sometimes sit for hours among the

**Above: If a puppy and a kitten grow up together they are usually as good friends as this young dog and kitten.**

high branches.

Cats cannot be taught tricks as dogs can. They cannot be made to do anything which they do not want to do. They are very independent.

It is a good idea for a cat-door to be fitted into the back door. It is a flap which the cat can push both ways. This lets the cat go in and out of the house as it pleases.

Lots of people think that cats never make friends with dogs. This is untrue. Once a cat and dog get used to each other they will live quite happily together.

**Below: A cat-flap allows your pet to come and go as it wishes.**

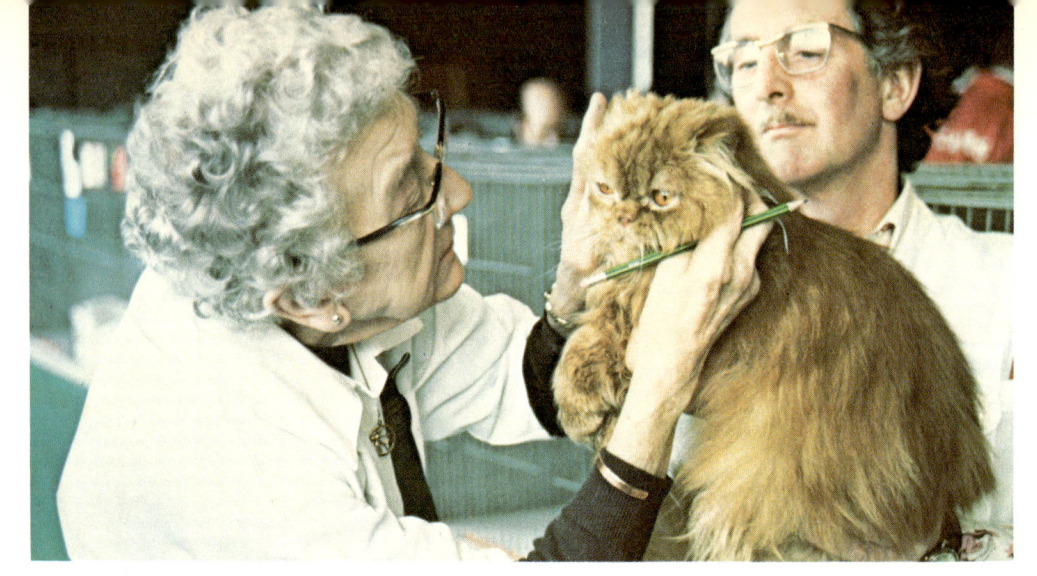

## 11 HEALTH AND CARE

**Above: Take your sick cat to a vet for treatment.**

**Below: All cats love to have their fur brushed as often as possible.**

It is very important to know how to look after a pet. A cat which is healthy will look bright and happy. Its fur will be glossy and its eyes clear. If a cat seems sick a vet will be able to tell what is wrong with it.

No pet will ever be healthy unless it is fed properly. A grown-up cat needs two meals a day. It will also want milk. There should always be a bowl of water where the cat can reach it easily.

The cat's fur should be brushed often. Long-haired cats need brushing every day. Cats will love it and will purr loudly while being brushed. Their fur should also be combed occasionally to get rid of the tangles and bits of dirt.

Cats keep their own coats clean, so they do not need baths as dogs do. When cats lick their coats they are helping to groom themselves. They take out any loose hair with their tongues. This hair collects in the cat's stomach and now and then the cat will cough it up.

Nearly all cats catch fleas at some time. The cat keeps scratching itself behind the ears and on its back. Flea powder gets rid of the fleas but the instructions must be read carefully. Its bedding should be changed as that is where the fleas lay their eggs.

**Above: Cats lick their coats to keep themselves clean.**

# 12  CAT FANCYING

Cats are the favorite pets of many people all over the world. People who love cats and who take great interest in everything about them are called "cat fanciers". Cat fanciers do not all agree on the best way to treat their cats.

Some like to give their cats a life of luxury. Their cats sleep on velvet cushions and are treated like babies. They eat only carefully prepared food which is cut into small pieces for them. Their owners think that a cat's stomach is easily upset.

These cats are not let out of doors

**Above: Cats that live a life of luxury can overeat and become fat.**

**Below: Some cat owners allow their pets to look after themselves.**

**Above: This cat's owner is treating it like a human by giving it a bed decorated with lace and soft fabric.**

**Below: These cats lead a tough, outdoor life during their stay in this cattery.**

if the weather is cold or damp. Their owners believe that they would catch a chill. Neither are they allowed out at night in case they get lost in the dark.

Other owners treat their cats very differently. Their cats are given large lumps of raw meat to tear and chew up for themselves. These owners will allow their cats out in all weathers. If the cats choose to stay away for a few nights the owners do not worry about their pets.

These people believe that it is best to let cats live as they did before they became domesticated thousands of years ago.

## 13 CAT SHOWS

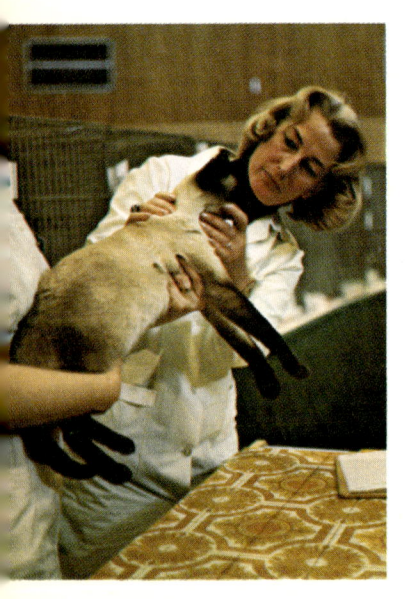

**Above: A vet checks if a cat is healthy before it is put on show.**

A cat which takes part in a cat show is a pedigree or purebred. This means that its parents and grandparents were all the same breed and were also pedigrees. Cat shows are held so that the finest cats in the world can be judged.

When the cats arrive at a show they are looking their very best. They look perfect. Their fur has been rubbed with Fuller's Earth to remove any dust or grease. Their ears, eyes and claws have also been cleaned.

A vet looks at every cat before the show to make sure that they are all healthy. Any cat which seems sick is

**Left: A pedigree cat enjoying a brushing by its proud owner before the start of the show.**

not allowed to enter the show.

Each cat is then put in a pen, the owners leave and the judges are called in. The judges look closely at the appearance of the cats. They notice health, shape and coloring and give points for each of these things. The judges also see how the cats behave. A nervous or bad-tempered cat will lose marks.

The cats which score most points are awarded certificates. These cats are the best of their breed and are called champions.

**Above: This bad-tempered cat will get few marks. Below: A champion cat with many of its prize rosettes.**

## 14  IN LEGENDS

One of the goddesses of the Ancient Egyptians was called Bast. She had the face and head of a cat, with whiskers and pointed ears. She was the goddess of pleasure and enjoyed music and dancing. The Egyptians believed that she protected them from illness.

Many years later the cat was thought of as an evil animal. In Europe witches were supposed to keep cats as their closest friends. Sometimes a cat was believed to be a witch in disguise. People came to

**Above: The cat-headed goddess, Bast.**

**Below: Cats were once believed evil, and often pictured with witches.**

look on cats as magic creatures which could do them harm.

At one time no sea journey would be started without the ship's cat on board. These cats were thought to protect the ship from storms. If there did happen to be a shipwreck, the cat would be among the first to be saved from the sinking ship.

In Belgium, Spain and the U.S.A. a white cat was believed to bring happiness to all who saw it. In Britain a black cat was a sign of good luck, but in other parts of Europe it was a sign of disaster.

**Below: If the ship was sinking, the ship's cat was saved first.**

# 15  FAMOUS PEOPLE'S CATS

There have been many famous people who have loved their pet cats very much.

One of these people was Dr Samuel Johnson, the famous English writer who lived in the 18th century. He owned a cat named Hodge who was very fond of oysters. Although Johnson had a servant, he would never send him out to buy the oysters. He thought the servant might dislike Hodge if he had to go out shopping for a cat. So, Johnson always bought Hodge's oysters.

Mohammed, who founded the

Moslem religion in the seventh century, loved cats. There is a story that a snake crawled into his sleeve and refused to leave. So, Mohammed's cat asked the snake to put its head out of the sleeve to have a chat. When the snake did so the cat seized it, pulled it from the sleeve and dragged it away.

There are other people who do not like the company of cats. Napoleon did not like being in the same room as one. He said that when a cat stared at him it made him feel a little scared.

**Above: Mohammed's cat caught the snake that had crawled up the prophet's sleeve and took it away.**
**Left: Dr Samuel Johnson sitting at his desk in his study with Hodge, nearby on a chair.**

# WORDS YOU MAY NOT KNOW

**Breed**  A group of cats which have the same general features.

**Certificate**  A document that gives written proof that a certain event has happened, such as when a champion cat is presented with the first prize.

**Champion**  The cat chosen as best in its breed out of all the cats put on show.

**Disaster**  A tragic event which leads to great suffering.

**Domesticated**  An animal that has been tamed and now is used to living with people.

**Evolve**  To change, over millions of years, from simple kinds of animals or plants into more complex forms.

**Independent**  Not dependent on anything or anyone.

**Pedigree**  Line of birth that can be directly traced through several generations, usually about eight.

**Prey**  Any animal that is hunted or killed by another animal for food.

**Stray**  An animal that is separated from its owner and now roams the streets.

**Vet**  An animal doctor.